The Teachings of

written by Henry Jean Carter

with illustrations by Sarah Curry

Wit Publishing
P.O. Box 221105
Beachwood, Ohio 44122

THE TEACHINGS OF MOTHER WIT
and
THE APPLE DOESN'T FALL FAR FROM THE TREE

FIRST EDITION

Library of Congress Catalog Card Number: 96-92386

10 9 8 7 6 5 4 2

ISBN 0-7880-0691-6

PRINTED IN THE U.S.A.

What they're saying about Mother Wit...

"*The Teachings of Mother Wit* summarizes for me, many of the survival skills that come from the wisdom and life long experiences of old folks. It is indeed refreshing to see these in print for young people to read and to grasp the understanding."

Clarence W. Mixon, Ph.D.
Unit Principal
Cleveland Heights High School

"Henry Jean Carter's book is excellent. It's like a trip back to a simple, caring, concerned and sharing time. As Scripture tells us '...you are the salt of the earth...' Mark 9: 49-50. This book reminds us of Jesus' words. Our ancestors lived them daily. We should too. Take this book with you everywhere. It is a great companion..."

Sr. Juanita Shealey
Executive Director
Catholic Interracial Council of Greater Cleveland

"*Mother Wit* represents a harkening back to the call of our ancestors. This is the new drum -- a call that also holds our measured responses to our sojourn here. *Mother wit* is our blues, our jazz, our song through the ages. Nothing but a closer harmony can come from this!"

James Spriggs
Teacher & Writer
Cleveland State University

"...I found myself immersed in the lessons... So many memories flooded my mind -- some bearing tears and other opening the gates of joy. ...remembering who had said these things to me as I was growing up, I came to appreciate my own mother and grandmother. This is time well spent... As principal of a middle school, I deal with adolescents daily. This will be a great tool for guiding these students. It is a great resource when working with their values, social skills and attitudes. This warm and sensitive book takes me back in time to fully appreciate the beauty of life through the eyes of every mother, including my own!"

Anna Maria Tabernik
Principal
Roxboro Middle School

"I am a 6th grade drop out. I was not able to attend school because my father died when I was 11 and mother's income was just $14.00 a month. So I worked odd jobs to help out. I raked leaves, picked cotton and stuff like that to earn a living and assist at home. My mother could not read or write but I learned from my sister and brother. I got a job working for LTV Republic Steel because I performed the tasks -- not based on education but on attitude and desire to do my part. Now retired after 40 years of service I am happy to see the wisdom I learned growing up is in a book. *Mother wit* taught me self pride and to earn, not steal from others or take what wasn't mine."

Elijah Hudson
A Maintenance Man, Retired
Cleveland, Ohio

"Some people think of *mother wit* as instinct, others as intuition. I think of mother wit as "Wisdom of the Soul" and no one has access to your soul but God. Call it what you want, but I call it a gift from God."

W. Faye Butts
Promotion Manager
13 WMAZ Television
Macon, Georgia

"There once was a lady who labored
on what is a book about love.
She shared her true thoughts about living
and the guidance we get from above.
We should share with our children these teachings
and live them ourselves. True Mother wit is life's wisdom.
God bless the author, Henry Jean Carter."

Abby Chizmar
Registered Nurse

"Book learning goes a long way but *Mother Wit* lasts forever."

Judge Una R. Keenon
East Cleveland Municipal Court

"Reading this book has been a thoroughly entertaining way to get my Ph.D. in living sensibly without attending college."

Karl McKenzie
Career Postal Worker
Cleveland Heights, Ohio

The teachings of... mother wit
The apple doesn't fall far from the tree.

Editor
Marv Gisser

Illustrations artwork
Sarah Curry

Book Design and Cover
Dicc Klann

"The Teachings of Mother Wit"
"The Apple Doesn't Fall Far From The Tree"
concept of right side pages only
created by
Henry Jean Carter
for enjoyable reading
and to be inviting to interested young people.

Book Cover
Author Concept

Apple Characters
created by the author

A Thank-You Note from the Author

The following deserve mention for their help and love in my efforts to publish this work:

More Marketing without Money by Nicholas E. Bade
Writing in Ohio, second edition by Lavern Hall
Ruth K. Brown & Janice Hocevar & Agnes Green,
Ted Schwarz, writer and consultant
Cleveland Heights Library and East Cleveland Library
for research purposes,
Friends, old and new ones,
Dr. M. Boswell,
Lea Leever Oldham, writer & teacher, Patricia Mote,
Joseph Taddeo, attorney
James Spriggs, categories consultant,
my proofreaders
and the many people I interviewed on the subject.
A bundle of support and courage from my co-workers
A very special thank-you to my husband,
and my mother,
for allowing me the time for myself to work hard
and do the best job I could.
Thanks to my daughter & sons who believe in my accomplishment.

If I missed someone, I am thanking you now,
with all sincerity.

And finally, I thank you, God
for allowing me to finish this work.
It is a gift to me and so many others who will read this book.
I truly praise God from whom all blessings flow.

What is Mother Wit?

Some call it common sense...or horse sense...or having enough sense to make the best decisions for yourself and others. When I was growing up, we called it *mother wit*.

Mother wit is a collection of well-known sayings, enhanced and expanded with personal commentary, inviting the reader to use his or her common senses — seeing, hearing, tasting, smelling and feeling. These senses, common to each and every one of us, are aimed at pin-sticking readers, sharply reminding them there are choices whenever decisions must be made.

Many of the *mother wit* sayings have a universal message to them and they apply equally to everyone. Chances are wherever you lived, a parent or grandparent or aunt or uncle admonished, warned, threatened, reminded and most important, taught you the value of *mother wit*; of using your common sense.

Today we hear a call for a return to basic values that families once lived by and instilled in their children. Unfortunately, that guidance seems to have been lost. Let this book be not only a reminder of simpler times, but also serve as a *guidebook* on the way to understanding life in the 21st century, without forsaking yesterday's values and common sense.

The commentaries suggest ways to avoid pitfalls and avoid unwise choices. We are more concerned with achievements and accomplishments. This book is not meant to be preachy or be a sermon. You might, however, call it our freewill offering.

This book is designed to help the reader examine the challenges in his or her life; to provide an *inspirational message of self-help* for each and every reader.

May it spank the brain and accelerate the mind with valuable purpose. If it serves to help some readers reach a new attitude and approach to life, the book has succeeded. If it helps some readers trash what has become a negative way of life, the book has succeeded.

Mother wit is itself a common sense piece of advice. Even though *mother wit* applies to everyone, the commentary in this book reflects only the author's interpretation. Your viewpoint may be different as a result of a different lifestyle, upbringing or attitude. The choice is yours. But you may want to heed some of the suggestions in this book.

I dedicate this book
to my children
and their children.

I also offer this special dedication
to all the grandparents
who have picked up the pieces
from dysfunctional homes
and, at great personal sacrifice,
are trying to keep their families together.

In loving memory
of R. E. Carter

Guide to Sayings

Appreciation and Beauty

Business and Your Job

Character and Personality

Choices and Consequences

Faith and Inspiration

Family and Parenting

Friendship and Love

Goals and Requirements

Knowledge and Truth

Life and Resolutions

Priorities and Structure

Relationships and Reality

Success and Prosperity

Thrift and Investment

Thoughts and Reflections

Appreciation and Beauty

Beauty is only skin deep.

The human body does not always reflect the best of nature's beauty. Often, we have a tendency to cover even the "good parts" with so much cosmetic enhancement that true physical beauty is hidden. But true beauty is within. It comes from the heart and soul and is determined by how you act toward your fellow human beings. To determine beauty, get to know a person's character and personality. Only then can you know how beautiful a person is.

You cannot pluck roses without fear of thorns.

The rose is a symbol of beauty. But its thorns can pierce if you don't handle it carefully. Even then, you may get pierced. *Mother wit* tells us it is no different with people. External appearances can be deceiving. Good looks may hide the sharp pricking of a person's thorny nature. Perhaps you know someone who reminds you of a beautiful rose, but who stuck you time and time again in personal encounters. You have to work them before they work you.

Light is greater in the darkness.

If your life seems to be in total darkness, look for the glow. Keep a vision that allows you to see things for what they really are. Don't accept darkness as a way of life. Your light can be God, your parents, a good friend, or anyone who helps shed hope when everything around you seems

dark. God is light. He will always be there for you and for everyone else. You only have to open your eyes to His light.

Memory is the power to gather roses in the winter.

Memory is the power to gather roses in the winter.

We should be thankful for memories. We can rewind the tape of our lives and selectively recall the past. Memories help us relive what was once a part of us, but now is gone. They rekindle the good times and the bad. They conjure up recollections of family and friends and events. Remembering yesterday helps us to go forward, even in the hardest of times. And on the coldest of days we can still recall the lovely scent of a rose and the glorious shade of red.

If you realize you are not as wise today as you thought you were yesterday, then you are wiser today.

It only takes a little personal evaluation to check where you've been in life. Even if you only learn that you're still circling around with the same old problems, you have made a valuable discovery. It's healthy to know where you have been and where you are now. If you have learned that, your *mother wit* has kicked in and you are wiser today.

Waste not, want not.

Don't be extravagant! Take care of what is yours, and use it to its best advantage. Don't be frivolous and wasteful with money or material items or even with food. If you take care of what you have, you will not have to worry as much about the future. A good part of *mother wit* is good stewardship of all we are given. Taking care today means tomorrow is more secure.

There is no cosmetic as beautiful as a happy person.

The glow that radiates from a happy person outshines any manufactured beauty product. Here is *mother wit* in action. Upbeat people create an aura of peacefulness that can be transmitted to others. It would be nice if happiness were as contagious as the common cold. Do your part to spread joy in this world.

There is no cosmetic as beautiful as a happy person.

It's a hard, sad life for many people, so don't scorn the simple things that give them pleasure.

There may be only one pleasure that keeps a person happy. We may think that pleasure worthless or foolish. We need to let those people alone if their pleasure is not

harmful to themselves and does not endanger others. Let them enjoy the simple pleasure if that's what they like doing. It's their life, not yours.

Don't judge a book by its cover.

Looks are deceiving. The person with the pretty face or handsome body may be ugly inside. The individual with looks that would never win a beauty contest may be beautiful inside. Then again, neither may be true. Get to know a person before making a value judgment about the kind of individual he or she is.

Don't judge a book by its cover.

I will honor each day in my heart.

We need not wait for our once-a-year birthday or anniversary or Valentine's Day to display our heart and feelings to others. We should celebrate and praise each other throughout the four seasons and give when our heart desires. Today is not too soon to let someone know how he or she is appreciated. Don't wait. A thank-you note is welcome at any time of the year. Your *mother wit* knows when to show your appreciation. Listen to that inner voice and act appropriately.

Business and Your Job

Go with the flow.

Going against the power structure will create problems for yourself. If you can't take orders, you will be punished. The power of the pen can hurt you for a long time. Written reprimands can ruin any chance for future advancement. Even worse, your fellow workers may snub you. If you can't afford to leave, and it's increasingly difficult to stay, learn to role play.

Pay the cost to be the boss.

If you are going to be in charge, eliminate all loose ends and remain in charge. There is a price to pay if you are going to run the show. You cannot half-step. You have to be able to say, "I paid for it. It's mine." And, "paid for," is not just dollars and cents. It is your hard work and your sweat and your labor. Then you will be in charge.

Pay the cost to be the boss.

He who cannot obey cannot command.

If you cannot be relied on to do something by a superior or peer, you are not considering others. Nor are you considering your own future. Be flexible about doing what is asked

of you. Then, when it is time for you to ask for assistance, others will be more willing to work with you. We all have to learn to work with others. It is to your advantage to learn how to do it, and do it well. Others will respect your requests. On the other hand, do not volunteer for a task for which you know you are not qualified. A poor result will not help you on life's pathway. Knowing your limitations is good *mother wit*.

A pat on the back, then a swift kick in the behind.

Once the job is done and your services no longer needed, your employer may decide to get rid of you. Unfortunately, too many times in this day and age you get very short notice and no explanation. Then comes this new, probably younger person, often with less experience who will work more cheaply. Use your *mother wit* and be prepared. Try to recognize the signs, and watch out for the "pink slip."

Many kiss the hand they wish to cut off.

In the working world, it may be necessary to go along with a boss or co-worker who is not easy to work with. It is even more difficult when you don't care for that person — or you know that person doesn't care for you. You may harbor negative feelings, but in order to maintain a productive workplace, you "go with the flow." It may not be the way you would like it, but that is the way it's done.

A company is known by the people it keeps.

We've all been told that "people are known by the company they keep." In today's marketplace, a company is

known by the people it keeps. The employees your company keeps tell a lot about your firm's goals. If the selection process is yours, be very careful about your choice of candidates for a particular job or assignment. Try to hire employees who will enhance your business. Once you hire them, improve their skills with workshops, on-the-job training, seminars and incentives. Your associates define the character of your business and your *mother wit* shows.

Are you looking for the man in charge or the woman who knows what's going on?

Are you looking for the man in charge or the woman who knows what's going on?

Perhaps there is a business owned by someone but the female employee runs the show. She knows exactly what is going on and she is reliable, dependable and loyal to her boss. Yet she is in control. He would probable say "see my secretary - - she knows how everything is run here. I'm here all the time but she runs the company." He is a wise man to honor her in her abilities and to trust that she does really know everything. He may be too busy to follow some of the small details. His *mother wit* tells him to rely on her. Her *mother wit* keeps her on her toes and valuable to her boss. It's a win - win situation.

Tough customers are still customers.

The world is made up of all kinds of people. Some you

can please; others you cannot, no matter what you do. Those you cannot please take special handling. A difficult customer might have been difficult before the two of you came in contact. If you are aware of this attitude from the beginning, you may be able to handle the situation more carefully. Remember that a customer's attitude is not always something you can do anything about. Their attitude is their problem, not yours! Keep your cool. The next customer could make your day.

It's not the number of hours you put in. It's how much you put in the hours.

As true as this is to life in general, in this case it refers to the world of work. Perhaps you were on the job for a full eight hours. Or perhaps you're proud of the fact you are always on time and never miss a day of work. All well and good, but that's just part of it. Were you productive? Was your work correct and accurate? Did you set a good example for your fellow workers? In other words, was your *mother wit* showing through? If you value your job and meet its demands, you will be rewarded.

It takes months to get a customer, seconds to lose one.

Don't tear down what you have built up. It takes months to get a customer and only seconds to lose one. (The same holds true for friends.) Even though you are providing customers a service, they feel they are supporting you by spending their money. Keep in mind how you feel when you are the customer. It is the golden rule of business and of *mother wit* -- treat them as you would want to be treated. It will keep them returning. Repeat customers always help a business succeed and flourish.

Character and Personality

An empty wagon makes a lot of noise.

The wise man keeps quiet and observes, listening and waiting for the right time to speak. Those who are neither wise nor filled with wisdom will talk excessively and like to be heard. They succeed only in revealing their foolishness to others. So don't make a lot of useless chatter. *Mother wit* says listen and learn.

Don't wear too many faces. You might forget which one you're wearing and embarrass yourself.

Don't wear too many faces. You might forget which one you're wearing and embarrass youreslf.

Halloween is not a year-'round holiday, even though some people keep masks on all the time. There may be times when you want to claim you are more than what you truly are. You will know that you are not telling the truth. The truth is the light, and it will shine. You can't fool people forever. The truth will rise, and you are only deceiving yourself. Your mask has to come off sometime. Show your *mother wit* and be yourself at all times with all people. There are no masks to hide the real you.

The ability to be silent when necessary is an important part of self-mastery.

Knowing when to talk and when not to is to your advantage. The fish wouldn't have been caught if he kept his mouth shut. Some people are the same. The wise person knows when to speak and when to listen. The ability to keep silent will put you in tune with the speaker.

Make sure your brain is in gear before operating your mouth.

Make sure your brain is in gear before operating your mouth.

Take time to think about what you want to say. Gather your thoughts and make sure of what you have in mind before you speak. Be certain your words are appropriate, clear, and not offensive. You don't want to regret something improper you may have said because you didn't think it through clearly first.

Better silent than sounding stupid.

Just because you are a good conversationalist does not mean you own the conversation. Do you let others get a word in? Do you talk ninety percent of the time? Do you listen? Do you alienate and bore others as you ramble on? Controlling a conversation, with little regard for others, does not guarantee one's intelligence.

A smile is a curve that can set a lot of things straight.

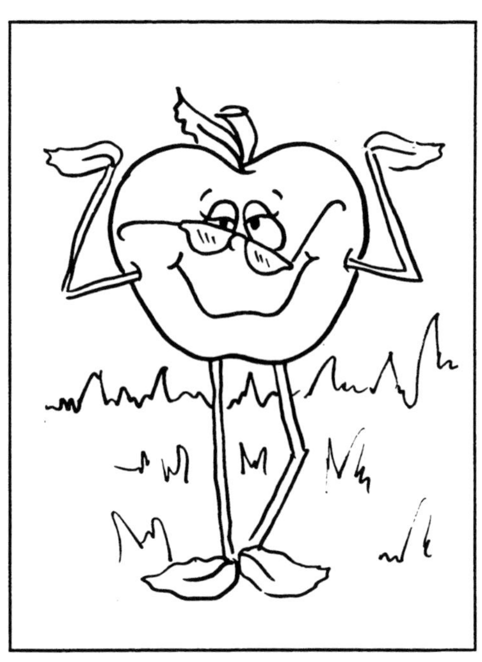

A smile is a curve that can set a lot of things straight.

Good eye contact may be there, and you may have a clear understanding of each other's words. Yet, you do not feel comfortable with the other party. Yet, as soon as a smile appears, the ice is broken. A rainbow smile can add warmth and hospitality. When you get that bit of communication, both parties can relate to each other a little bit better. A genuine smile is a gentle, non-verbal way to add to your character.

Act the way you'd like to be, and soon you will be the way you act.

This can be a positive or negative situation. Only you can create and control your character and personality. Stay in good standing and stand for something good. Be a valuable person in your home and community. Value your reputation. Don't just become known as a good person. Become one! You will reap the benefits.

Walk softly but carry a big stick.

Don't brag about yourself, letting everyone know how great and fantastic you are. Be soft-spoken and detail-minded. You don't have to make a lot of noise to express

who and what you are. People know a soft-spoken, quiet-on-the-outside person can harbor a stormy interior. Keep that calm, and use the storm to your advantage. Control it; don't let it control you.

It's nice to be important, but it's important to be nice.

You own this. You have that. But let's face it, you are not a very nice person. You're hard to get along with, or you're a grouch. Most people appreciate a nice person, rather than one who is grumpy. How would you like to go through life—respected and appreciated—or friendless?

The rooster thought the sun rose to hear him crow.

The rooster thought the sun rose to hear him crow.

Just like the cock that thinks it controls the sunrise, there are people who think they are the sole reason things happen. Whether they want to believe it or not, the show will go on without them. Ask yourself, "Will things function normally without me?" "Would certain things have happened if I had not been there?" Answer honestly, and depending on your answer, feel free to crow at 5 a.m. tomorrow and wake your neighbors. That is, if you think your *mother wit* would let you. Most of us know we are not indispensable and show gratitude instead of ego.

He who makes excuses accuses himself.

Don't use weak excuses to explain why you did not do what you were supposed to do, especially when you are in a responsible position and others depend on you. Any explanation must be clear and reasonable to the listener. Your reasoning may make all good sense to you, but not to anybody else. In fact, don't make excuses. Fulfill your obligation, whatever it is. When you don't fulfill your obligation, and come up with an excuse -- an alibi -- it affects other people, too. As much as we try, however, there will be times when an obligation is not fulfilled. A legitimate excuse may be acceptable, but don't make a habit of it.

Make yourself a sheep and eventually you will meet a wolf.

If you are non-resistant and have no defense to protect yourself, if you let most anyone into your life, if you are easily manipulated -- you can be sucked up as if by a vacuum cleaner. Not everyone who comes your way is good. You might be hurt. Wrongdoers look for a sheep, the good-natured target to prey on. Everybody you meet is not a con artist, but unfortunately there are enough of them looking for the sheep that you have to protect yourself at all times.

Make yourself a sheep and you will eventually meet a wolf.

That doesn't mean you have to change your personality or way of life. It means you have to protect yourself. Don't let just anyone into your heart—or your pocket.

Time heals all wounds, but only you can keep the scars from showing.

If your wounds have physically healed, but you have not healed emotionally, you are still traumatized. You will appear to others to be a troubled person. Find some means of recovery. Make a wise investment with your life, create a new outlook, or make a move away from the past, mentally and physically. Add a permanent-press smile to your new life. If you smile, perhaps most of the world will smile with you. The battle scars will remain, but you can change your life for the better. If time does not heal, then seek the best counseling you can find.

Anger often is more harmful than the injury that causes it.

Pushed to the edge, you will lose your patience and then your ability to reason. *Mother wit* says you must stay in control. But do not let your anger remain bottled up, because you can explode. That could lead to destruction of some kind. The matter can be much smaller than the damage you could allow it to do.

Sticks and stones may break your bones, but words will never hurt you.

This was true years ago, but times have changed. Words can hurt because we have become a society that will sue. Now we can be sued for slander or libel, so words can hurt

you. We should never verbally abuse people of any age. People's feelings are alive, and we must not slander them—or what they perceive as slander—any more than we would physically abuse them. Awareness of the power of words is more obvious now than ever.

Watch how you handle people. They are not things or objects. A lawsuit could be in your face. People may forgive, but they don't always forget.

The best remedy for a short temper is a long walk.

A short temper can get you into trouble. Too often, we don't think before we act or react. A walk can serve as a cooling-off process and give us an opportunity to think, a chance to evaluate the situation. Asking for spiritual guidance is another method to control that temper. *Mother wit* suggests time out for short tempers.

Sometimes you can't tell if someone is wearing a halo or horns.

Be careful not to be deceived by others' personalities and characters. A person's outward actions may seem a far cry from the reality. Bear in mind there are two types of communication, verbal and non-verbal. Listen to the words but watch the body. A smile is not always a smile, and

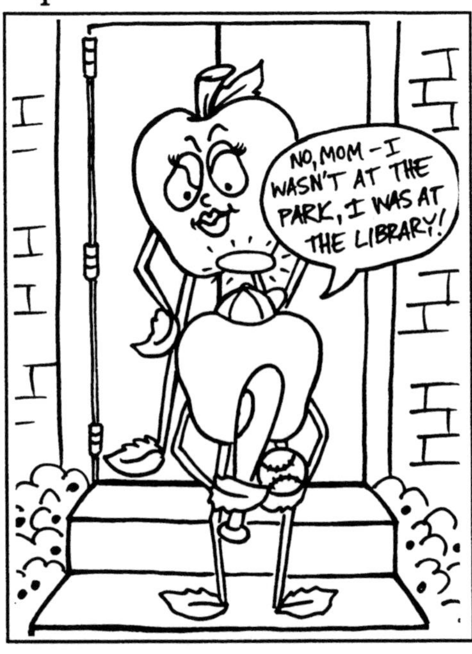

Sometimes you can't tell if someone is wearing a halo or horns.

we've all heard of crocodile tears. Be careful how you perceive others and even more careful of how you are perceived.

A man is about as big as the things that make him angry.

A man is about as big as the things that make him angry.

Getting angry at the smallest crisis only proves your own limitations. If you have a tendency to get upset about the least little thing, work on your tolerance, understanding, and decision-making. Work, also on your acceptance of others. Improving these will help you make wiser responses and saner judgments. Using your *mother wit* you will become a better person.

Choices and Consequences

Today's menu — Two choices: Take it or leave it.

Set ground rules for yourself. Take a firm stand. There will be circumstances when you have to give someone a choice. This works well when you are trying to sell something or are negotiating with someone. It is very simple to understand what you want to do. There are no gray areas. Take it or leave it!

Today's menu -- Two choices: Take it or leave it.

Live by the sword, die by the sword.

Individuals whose lives center around a primary habit and become obsessed with something they cannot control or step away from destroy themselves. The most extreme result is death! This does not always mean drugs. Are you following your doctor's advice about certain foods that have a negative effect on you? Still smoking? Let go of those habits that can and will destroy you. Always evaluate the things that, or the people who, influence you strongly and cause attachments. Look around in your family and friends. See who is showing good *mother wit*. Make certain you pick the right role model or you will live by the sword, die by the sword. Lose those bad habits and nurture your life with goodness.

When the cat's away, the mice will play.

When the cat's away, the mice will play.

Just because a parent, boss or someone in authority is not in attendance is no reason to act any differently from the way you would act if they were present. *Mother wit* asks us to act honorably at all times. We all know the world is full of people who are more than glad to wait until the person in charge returns and then report everyone's actions except their own. If you honor your internal conscience, this will never be the dog that bites you on the tail.

It's a poor rat that has only one hole.

Don't go through life with a one-way ticket. Have another way back to where you began, or be able to move on. Keep yourself out of situations in which you owe others. Have a backup financial source to help you through the bad times.

There is always free cheese in a mouse trap.

A "free" gift may have a lot of strings attached. There could be a hidden cost that will cause you a great deal of grief. The statement used to be, "There's no such thing as

a free lunch." It still holds true. And *mother wit* does not allow us to be looking for the free lunch. Be responsible. Don't get caught in a trap, and don't trap yourself.

Don't make a mountain out of a molehill.

Deal with things just as they are. Don't make more of something than there is. We all need to understand the difference between a problem and a disaster. We face problems on a daily basis, but can get back on line by using good judgment. A problem may seem large, but it's still a molehill. *Mother wit* says don't make it more than it is. A disaster strikes unexpectedly and has devastating results. It could take months or years to recover. Don't underestimate such a problem. It's tough to climb to the top of the mountain. Be aware of your daily molehills and irregular mountains. Be prepared to cope with them. Don't overreact.

Don't make a mountain out of a molehill.

If you can't stand the heat, get out of the kitchen.

Constant conflict, never-ending problems, gaining acceptance. You're the target of ongoing criticism. These all weigh heavily on you. Sound familiar? If this describes your life, maybe it's time to move on. Check your *mother wit* and take a fresh approach to life.

Change with the times unless you are big enough to change the time.

Don't dwell on the past and make statements about "the way it used to be." Change with the times. Go back to school. Learn a new skill. Redecorate your home and reform your life. Relocate! You cannot stop time. Every day is a new adventure with new products and new ideas. *Mother wit* offers a whole new outlook. Take advantage of the new and don't live in the past.

Let sleeping dogs lie.

Don't look for trouble. If things are going along smoothly, don't try to find a reason to cause problems. That's not good *mother wit*. When you have no real reason to take an action except to see someone else's reaction, you create as many, if not more, difficulties for yourself than for the person who reacts.

Let sleeping dogs lie.

Don't do the crime if you can't do the time.

For every crime you commit, you will suffer. If you're caught, you may be locked up in an institution. If you're not caught, you still will suffer. Your conscience will bother you, and you'll always be looking over your shoulder. Either way, you will do time. To spend your time worrying about not being caught is as wasteful and nonproductive as being caught and locked away.

Two men looked out from prison. One saw mud, the other saw stars.

Each person has a vision. The one who saw mud was looking down at his life. His head was not turned in the right direction, toward positive change. That is the direction *mother wit* would have offered. The other one who saw stars, because he had his head up, had hope. When you walk with your head down, you don't see the world or what there is to accomplish. We must see the whole picture in order to make a difference. With your head up, walking tall, you face the challenge to redo your life. And what you do to improve your own life also improves the lives of everyone you come into contact with.

Leave no stone unturned.

Once you have an instinct that a situation is not quite right, take inventory. Examine the situation to determine what isn't right. Continue to examine and search for what's wrong. Use your *mother wit.* Don't quit until you're totally satisfied you have the answer -- the right answer. Don't think you are sure. Be very sure. Look at all the possibilities inside and out.

Face the music, even if you don't like the tune.

Accept things as they are, even if you don't like the arrangement. Too often in life, we have little or no input in decisions that affect us, whether at home, on the job, or even in our leisure activities. Unfortunately, there are times when we have go along with the decisions of our family, company management, or the majority. When you

can, make your feelings known and be sure to emphasize your points. But confrontation is not the way of *mother wit*. Even though we are unhappy with the way things run, we have to learn to make the best of it. In the long run, it might prove to be the right arrangement after all.

You can't keep trouble from coming, but don't give it a chair to sit in.

Iron out your problems. Get a handle or solution on them. The one thing you really don't want to do is to ignore them and pretend they are not there. Don't stuff them away in your mind because the problems will certainly remain there. Deal with them and resolve them or make a settlement. The bottom line is to never welcome problems or become content and let them settle like dust. Put your resolutions together—let your ideas become like a vacuum cleaner—get rid of the dust, so life can go on.

You can't fit a square peg in a round hole.

Many times persons, places and things will not be compatible or just won't work together. If you see that something is unsafe, red flag it. Stop the job. Put up the "out of order" sign. Take responsiblity for the best outcome. And don't try to make something work that just isn't right. Use the correct tool for the job. There are consequences for not putting out your best. If you feel that something could be wrong, trust your instincts and your intuition. Better that than to regret some type of failure or disaster. Look to your *mother wit* for guidance when things just don't seem to be operating properly or if they leave any doubts in your mind.

Faith and Inspiration

When God is with you, it is better than the whole world being against you.

When God is with you, it is better than the whole world being against you.

Through God all things are possible. He has the power to change things when all seem to be against you. Remember God is an army; trust Him. He will guide and protect you. Prayer changes things. Make your mind aware and look for His signal. God has a way of letting us know He is there in spirit. Listen for that still small voice. You will see and feel His results.

When in trouble, one remembers God —whatever one calls Him.

Your contact with your God should not be limited to when you are in trouble. Thank Him for your blessings. If you think you have no blessings, just look around. You will see them. Be glad if you have your health and strength. Thank Him when things are going well. Love Him by doing good work and deeds. You will see the results of goodness through others' appreciation. God will lighten your heart in a special way. His shoulders are very broad. And remember that *mother wit* is having faith that things will

work out for the best in the long run if we let them go according to God's Holy plan. His is really the only plan that will work.

The Lord sometimes takes us into troubled waters, not to drown, but to clean us.

Sometimes a person gets into serious trouble time and time again, always promising never to go in that direction again. God will see this person through, but again he or she may have the same problem and end up in prison. Many times after an inmate has first-hand experience with a catastrophe, he or she will turn to Christianity. They wish to cleanse their hearts and souls of the corruptible ways of the past. Many individuals hold fast to this rebirth of the spirit.

God delays, but He doesn't forget.

God knows our needs, and He hears everyone's prayers. He remains our friend when others have walked out. He is everywhere, on call around the clock. We rejoice in knowing this. But if we are not sincere when we ask for His help, our prayers may not be answered. When this happens, the problem is ours, not His. We must remember always to pray, "Not my will, Father, but yours."

Live all the days of your life one at a time.

The future is not ours to see. We don't know what the road of life has in store for us. Live as though you expect God to visit you at any time of the day or night. You don't want to tell him, "Excuse me, I have a few things to pick up in my house. It's out of order. Can you want a minute?" Live life in such a way that you don't hurt anyone, you

don't owe any apologies or regret something you said or did. This is a starting point. You will think of your own personal reasons to live one day at a time. Life does not promise us anything; all we can do is work for the best. Don't hide problems away in your mind because, like dust bunnies under the bed, they will certainly remain there. Our *mother wit* tells us to deal with them, resolve them, or make a settlement.

If you fall down, it's better to fall on your back. If you can look up, you might want to get up.

If you fall on your face, you might not get up or even want to get up. With your face in the ground you will feel down and defeated. But if you land on your back, you will be able to look up and see things as they are. If you can face life as it is, you probably will envision a better way to reconstruct things for yourself. Lying flat on your back and looking wide-eyed at the world will get you back in touch with God. You will appreciate God and the many worldly things you previously just took for granted. Get up from your fall, whether it is a physical or mental one. Don't let it be a fall from grace.

If God lived on this earth, someone would break his window.

If God lived on earth, an enormous number of people would try to make contact with Him. They would knock on His door twenty-four hours a day. Not only would they break His windows, they would trample each other as they got in one another's way. We must remember that "Faith is the evidence of things not seen." If God is to dwell on earth, it must be in your heart.

The following biblical injunctions of faith are appropriate to this book. They stand alone and need no commentary. These are examples of the author's learnings that she was encouraged to learn by heart as a child. These became some of the foundation of her understanding of how things work. These are spiritual mother wit from the Holy Bible (King James Verson).

But thou art God, ready to pardon, gracious and merciful, slow to anger, and of great kindness. Nehemiah 9: 17

It is better to give than to receive.

Fear of the Lord is the beginning of knowledge, but fools despise wisdom and instruction.
Job 28: 28

Ask, and it shall be given you; seek, and ye shall find; knock, and it shall be opened unto you. For every one that asketh receiveth; and he that seeketh findeth; and to him that knocketh it shall be opened. Luke 11: 9,10

When I was a child, I spake as a child, I understood as a child, I thought as a child: but when I became a man, I put away childish things. I Corinthians 13: 11

The following biblical injunctions of faith may inspire you to additional reading.

The Ten Commandments:

Thou shalt have no other gods before me.

Thou shalt not make unto thee any graven image, or any likeness of any thing that is in heaven above, or that is in the earth beneath, or that is in the water under the earth:

Thou shalt not bow down thyself to them, nor serve them: for I the Lord thy God am a jealous God, visiting the iniquity of the fathers upon the children unto the third and fourth generation of them that hate me;

And shewing mercy unto thousands of them that love me, and keep my commandments.

Thou shalt not take the Lord thy God in vain; for the Lord will not hold him guiltless that taketh his name in vain.

Remember the sabbath day, to keep it holy.

Six days shalt thou labour, and do all thy work:

But the seventh day is the sabbath of the Lord thy God; in it thou shalt not do any work, thou, nor thy son, nor thy daughter, thy manservant, nor thy maidservant, nor thy cattle, nor thy stranger that is within thy gates:

For in six days the Lord made heaven and earth, the sea, and all that in them is, and rested the seventh day: Wherefore the Lord blessed the sabbath day, and hallowed it.

Honour thy father and thy mother: That thy days may be long upon the land which the Lord thy God giveth thee.

Thou shalt not kill.

Thou shalt not commit adultery.

Thou shalt not steal.

Thou shalt not bear false witness against thy neighbour.

Thou shalt not covet thy neighbour's wife, nor his manservant, nor his maidservant, nor his ox, nor his ass, nor any thing that is thy neighbour's.

Exodus 20: 3-17

The Lord's Prayer

Our Father which art in heaven, Hallowed be thy name.

Thy kingdom come. Thy will be done in earth, as it is in heaven.

Give us this day our daily bread.

And forgive us our debts, as we forgive our debtors.

And lead us not into temptation, but de-

liver us from evil: For thine is the kingdom, and the power, and the glory, for ever. Amen.

Matthew 6:9-13

The Twenty-third Psalm

The Lord is my shepherd; I shall not want.

He maketh me to lie down in green pastures: he leadeth me beside still waters.

He restoreth my soul: he leadeth me in the paths of righteousness for his name's sake.

Yea, though I walk through the valley of the shadow of death, I will fear no evil: for thou art with me; thy rod and thy staff they comfort me.

Thou preparest a table before me in the presence of mine enemies: thou anointest my head with oil; my cup runneth over.

Surely goodness and mercy shall follow me all the days of my life: and I shall dwell in the house of the Lord for ever. *Psalms 23*

Use the space below to put in your favorite expressions of faith. They may be from any source, not just your Bible. Mother wit is wisdom from many resources.

Family and Parenting

The apple doesn't fall far from the tree.

Being human, we sometimes question the actions and ways of family members. Why do some succeed and others fail? We raise questions about their character and behavior, and even their lifestyles, if they're not the same as ours. Why do they drink? Why do they keep getting in trouble with the law? Why do they keep arguing with each other? Why do they abuse one another? Many of these negative aspects are part of our family tree. Many of these traits were picked up by children just following what they saw or heard their parents doing. After all, if it's OK for parents to carry on this way, why can't we? The next time you are wondering why a youngster is behaving in a certain way, check the family history and social environment. The real story may be there.

The apple doesn't fall far from the tree.

You can fool most of the people some of the time, and some of the people all of the time — but you can't fool Mom.

Mom—or the mother figure in your life—has a great deal of powerful wisdom: She listens, is instinctive, sensi-

tive, and wise. She shields you with her love, and loves you even when others find you are no longer lovable. The look in your eyes goes directly to her heart, hurting when you hurt, happy when you are happy, sad when you feel pain. This is one place where every mother has *mother wit*.

Behind every good woman is a good man.

Behind every good woman is a good man.

This is equally valid the opposite way. Most females want the male's support of their decisions before they put them into motion. Too often, however, the male will say, "It's okay with me. Do what you want." That is not the answer most women want to hear. They want the male partner to be more supportive, mentally and physically. Men, be honest! If you see your partner going too far out on a limb, warn her, "Don't go." A male with good sound judgment and strength is very welcome to most females.

No success in life can make up for failure in the home.

Home is first in this ball game. Habits, manners, personality, character—all begin here. Outline a continuous teaching method for your children, and include spiritual teaching. Paint the best picture. Be supportive and make

time to monitor those children. Listen to them, and you will know if they have learned their home rules. Correct them, and hold the reins firmly. Your best *mother wit* is consistency. Don't waver in your efforts to raise them well. It works when all other functions fail and shut down. When you cry, you want to cry tears of joy, not tears of sorrow.

I am the man of the house and not the boy.

The one who truly is in charge of his home usually has his wife assist with responsibilities. (The reverse also is true.) He makes decisions and demonstrates authority, although at home he speaks in a soft voice. Members of the family support his style of positive leadership and lean on his shoulder to learn from him as he shares his wisdom. This is a father's place to demonstrate *mother wit*.

I am the man of the house and not the boy.

Once a man, twice a child.

Early in life, you are a child who is not able to take care of yourself. You depend upon parents, other family members or caring adults. Later, as a full-grown adult, you are able to provide the necessary shelter, clothing, food, and income. Still later, you mature into a senior adult. As in your early life, once again you may require aid. You are

retired or close to it. Your capabilities and your health may be declining. Assistance may be necessary once more, this time, from family, friends, or governmental agencies. As a youngster receiving help, you may not have known how to express your thanks. Now, be a gracious recipient and accept the benefits you have stored away for yourself with gratitude.

Mama and Papa, don't give away my plate and my bed.

The time may come when you may need a place to stay because of a crisis in your own home. It could be a lost lease or a lost argument. Have an understanding with your parents, when you first leave home, that you are going out on your own to do the very best you can. You are going to work, take care of yourself and become a responsible adult. But, let your parents know if good luck turns, you would like to come home until you get back on your feet. If this happens, be willing to help out any way you can, even if you can't shoulder much financial responsibility. You no longer are a child living under your parents' roof, but a thoughtful, caring adult. Here's a chance to show your parents that you have learned from their *mother wit* teachings.

Mama and Papa, don't give away my plate and my bed.

Friendship and Love

Never contend with a person who has nothing to lose.

This person may seem harmless, but will take you for everything you have. This type of person has nothing to lose, so if you lose, the fall will harm you a great deal more. Let these people go on their way. You will be better off without them.

Love thy neighbor, but don't take down the fence.

Certainly you would like to establish a "Hello, how are you?" relationship with your neighbor, perhaps even visit when it's convenient for both of you. But not all neighbors are interested in having an everyday relationship. When you start getting into another's home and start lending and borrowing, someone is going to blow it. Then comes the falling out. You stop speaking to each other. Short visits make longer friendships. Keep your fence up simply by saying "hi" and " 'bye." It works well for the majority of friend-and-neighbor relationships.

No news is good news.

If you haven't heard from relatives, friends, or business associates recently, maybe everything is going well. If there is trouble, chances are you'll be notified. But if nothing is going on, there is no protocol that indicates anyone —family or friend—must get in touch to let you know that everything is okay. You may be required by law to make contact in certain situations, but that is the exception rather

than the rule. It would be considerate, however, if people who are going away for a long time would leave a phone number or address behind to curb the "worrying syndrome." Even though we think everything is okay, it's nice to have it verified.

Live and let live.

Greed is wrong. That simple statement could change our lives. We need to share and give to others, not keep everything for ourselves. Perhaps when you get to the top, you can reach down and pull someone else up. But when you do pull someone up, don't expect a great deal in return. Let the deed be its own reward. It is just plain good use of your *mother wit* and as the Bible tells us, "It is more blessed to give than to receive."

People who live in glass houses shouldn't throw stones.

Be careful how you treat others, what you do to them and what you say about them. Too often, we ignore the fact we are not perfect. We forget the negative things about ourselves, our loved ones, family and even close friends. Remember the biblical injunction, "He that is without sin among you, let him first cast a stone at her." We cannot accuse another when we may be just as guilty.

Give an inch, one will take a mile.

We all know people who overextend privileges and take advantage of opportunities. They don't know when to stop. They push ever further, refusing to accept what has been offered. They finally reach the point at which no one will

extend them even the most minimal courtesy because they will take advantage of it and ask for more. That's not very good *mother wit*.

It is better to light one small candle than to curse the darkness.

Just a small amount of light gives us a good, safe, happy feeling. The average person wants to be in the company of light. Dark, brooding people prefer the dark. Light is protection against some of our fears and loneliness. Where there is light, there is hope and a feeling of security.

The best mirror is an old friend.

The best mirror is an old friend.

True friends can honestly tell you the truth. They can tell you whether you have done right or wrong. They have watched how you have coped over a period of time. They will reflect on your actions. Ask them to help you see through those things you are not certain of. You cannot see yourself as others can. Be willing to listen to their image of you. And be a good friend in return. This is *mother wit* in practice that will never let you down.

Scratch my back, I'll scratch yours.

There will be a time—or times—when you need a favor.

There is nothing wrong with that, it happens to all of us. You might have to call on a relative or good friend to lend you a helping hand. The person you seek help from will have the ability to help you achieve your quest. At some later time, the person who helped you might need your assistance. It's your turn to return the favor. "You help me, and I will help you." This is a good, solid practice that is successful in many personal and business relationships. And it's good use of your *mother wit*.

Lie down with a dog, you'll get up with fleas.

Watch those you hang around with. Check out their backgrounds. Make sure they are the kinds of people who are good enough to be called "friend." In many cases, you will inherit their good points and positive attitudes. But you can also inherit their faults, bad habits, problems, and even their reputation. These attitudes will rub off on you, and you will find yourself very much a part of their group. If they are unworthy of your friendship, you will become corrupt and regret associating with them.

Keep old friends and old roads.

Go where you are comfortable and around people who know you, and you will feel welcome if you are in need. Most likely these old friends will recognize your need and do something about it. If you tread in new territory among strangers, chances are very good you will be alone and probably not safe. Strangers will not feel comfortable with you because yours is an unfamiliar face. You may not mean any harm to them, but they do not know that; nor will they respond to your needs. There are certainly exceptions, but it's best to stick with people who know and care about you.

Take a long walk off a short pier.

Take a long walk off a short pier.

If you hear these words, you have either hurt or angered someone or caused him or her to mistrust you. They want you to walk away and never return. You are being told, "Drown, if you will. I don't care for you." This is a curtain-drawn relationship; the end of the show. Realize that it's over and get on with your life out of theirs.

Why buy the cow when you can get the milk free?

If a relationship has no morals, people are free to do as they please and ask for what they want without any commitment on their part. There is no plan to bond as one and share each other's needs as well as desires. You run the risk of not getting your partner to become united in marriage if everything is free and available. Have some expectations that work toward keeping a reputable character. Act honorably and make good choices. Listen to that intuition of yours, your *mother wit*, and act accordingly. Share your life with someone who loves these qualities about you and bond in a faithful way.

Don't wear your heart on your sleeve.

If you are timid, easily hurt, and take a long time to

heal, save yourself headaches by not revealing your true feelings. Life's reality is that all people we meet are not genuine, not compatible with us. Their values and morals may be different, and they are not grateful to be a part of us. They seem to think we owe them our hearts and souls. As a result, they will try to step all over us. We need to protect our feelings by extending them gradually, and then only to those with whom we are comfortable. Sometimes *mother wit* is just good caution.

Don't thank me. Pay me.

Don't thank me. Pay me.

It is best to make sure the favor you ask a friend to give you is free of charge. Have the courtesy to ask the other person if you can pay or tip them. Take nothing for granted, and do not assume anything. Assumptions have ruined many a friendship.

Friends are like precious metal: Gold—an old friend; silver—a new friend, and bronze—an acquaintance.

Long-time friends are like pieces of gold. Those you have known for a short time are like silver. The ones you have met recently, or see occasionally by chance, are like bronze. Friends are precious metals. If you have some that

are like gold, hang on to them. *Mother wit* opens the senses to people who are genuine. And sometimes acquaintances become good friends -- and the silver turns into gold.

Notes for the reader.

At different intervals within this book we have offered these open pages for your special notes and comments. Feel free to add your favorite quotations here as they relate to the chapters you have read.

Goals and Requirements

There are two things to aim for in life: To get what we want and then to enjoy it.

We constantly hear the word, **Goals.** Underline it, because goals will always be part of your life. Or should be. Highlight it in bright red letters in your mind. Depend upon it to see you through. To achieve your goals can be a little easier if you consider two aspects, long-term and short-term. Long-term goals are just that. They cannot be achieved in weeks or months. They may take a long time to achieve. Short-term goals, on the other hand, may not be quite as involved, and can be accomplished sooner. If you do not think you can achieve your goals on your own, work with a parent, friend or professional to establish your goals and how you plan to achieve them. Once you are set, move forward with determination. There will be plenty of hard work. There will be times you want to quit, but think of the proverbial pot of gold at the end of the rainbow. That is your goal. Like a pot of gold, it may be material wealth. But it could just as easily be happiness, satisfaction and joy.

There are no shortcuts to any place worth going.

Expect to work hard and spend long hours on any worthwhile project. Keep a positive outlook. Make a favorite project one of your priorities, even if it doesn't seem to blend in with your other activities. The time you invest will be worth all of the effort and struggle you put into your work. The reward will come later.

Do not follow the well-trod path. Blaze your own trail.

Create your own direction. Just because someone else chooses a particular course is no reason for you to follow in those footsteps. Think for yourself. Act on your own! Do what you judge is best for you. Be a leader! Blazing your own trail may just add some wonder and adventure to your journey as well.

If you snooze, you lose.

Be alert, no matter what is going on around you. Don't daydream or be in a fog. Look around you. There is a time to think and a time to be attentive. If you are in a trance, opportunities will pass you by.

If you snooze, you loose.

Kill two birds with one stone

Value your time and take advantage of it. Build on one achievement to improve another. Don't always look at one particular goal, but determine how that goal can help you lead and direct you toward another.

It's all right to have a train of thought, but you also need a terminal.

Have a lot of ideas that need action? It's not always

easy to get everything done. Don't overload your mind so much that you lose the ideas you had a year ago and have had on hold all this time. You will have to sift through your accumulated ideas and separate the wheat from the chaff. Be very realistic about what you can or cannot do. That's your terminal -- your *mother wit*. You have finally pulled your mind up to a stopping point to unload some of your thoughts.

What you confess, you possess.

If you want to improve your life, tell yourself, "Every day I am changing." Pack it into your mind, your heart, your soul. Let it be heard by those who will come to believe in you. They could give you a helping hand. Always promote the positive. When you say "can't," you probably are right. You can't! And you won't! You might try saying "I haven't yet..." or "I'll give it my best..." because then you leave the door open for the possibility of success. When you say "I can," and "I will," and "I am doing it," and "I have achieved," you probably are right again. Let the positive penetrate your entire being. Stay on top of your life. That's positive *mother wit* at its very best.

Don't let your left hand know what the right hand is doing.

Store away some information. Don't be eager to discuss all of your business. If you give away your plans, others may beat you to the finish line with your idea. Don't believe everyone is good-hearted. There are those who have no concerns about taking someone else's ideas and presenting them as their own to help them get ahead. Don't give away the recipe. It might be a prize winner.

Dead fish can float downstream, but it takes a live one to swim upstream.

Don't let life defeat you. Have a purpose in life. Go upstream in life, not downstream. If you want to succeed, you'll need a lot of energy and determination. Put your heart and soul into getting where you wish to be. Pay attention to your audience to determine if you are growing. This will send a strong message to others that you are doing what is necessary to move in the right direction which is upstream.

Knowledge and Truth

Everyone is ignorant—
only on different subjects.

Face it. You don't know everything! None of us does. No matter how educated you are, you will fall short in some areas. We all do. Ignorance only means you are not informed about a particular subject. Education can update you. Many have become great teachers or conversationalists after discovering -- and admitting -- they were lacking in some areas. It doesn't mean you are stupid. It does mean you don't have to pretend you know something that you really don't. Good *mother wit* is choosing to learn, not to remain in the dark.

If you can't see your way out,
feel your way.

Don't know how to get out of a difficult situation? If you know the timing is not right, and don't know where to turn or how to start, you will have to feel your way out. Work on your inner feelings. Do your best to resolve the problem reasonably and gradually. Use common sense, careful thinking and planning. Seek advice from someone whose judgment you trust, but make certain that judgment applies positively to you.

We tend to believe those we do not know
because they never have deceived us.

It is those polished, well-mannered, best-behaved individuals who influence us into believing "first-timers" are

just wonderful. But as time passes, and we get to know each other, the real, true colors emerge. Only then does the veil of pretense fall, and we get an accurate picture. The deception is over.

A stumble may prevent a fall.

Nobody can honestly say he or she never stumbled over something while walking. All of a sudden, you lose your balance and almost fall. It's an "almost" fall. The stumble prevented you from falling. If you make a mistake in thoughts or actions and stumble, try not to fall. You have a chance to regain your balance and get back in control. Take care of your life. It's not always possible to avoid catastrophes and problems. If they trip you up, watch your step and accept the stumble. It can prevent a serious fall.

If you tell the truth from the beginning, you don't have to remember anything.

If you tell the truth from the beginning, you don't have to remember anything.

When you tell a story, there are certain things others listen for. One is repetition. Are you repeating the story exactly the same way each time? There will be some discrepancies, but do you have times, dates, and places the same? The truth flows, but a liar fumbles and can't remember details. This is very important when you're filling out job or

credit applications. Some questions may reappear in a different version on a different line to determine if you are telling the truth. If you don't remember what you wrote on the application, a face-to-face interview will get to the truth very quickly. If you're paying attention to your *mother wit* you will know that the truth holds true and the false falls apart right before your eyes (or someone else's eyes).

All truths need not be told.

There are some secrets, some bits of information, that could cause terrible damage if revealed. There are occasions when telling the entire truth could create overwhelming heartache, alienate a great many people, and create a great deal of stress. Another saying, "What you don't know won't hurt you," certainly is appropriate here. We all have physical and mental skeletons in our closets. Let them stay there. There are times, however, when you can help someone by coming forward with the truth, the whole truth. If you listen to your intuition, your *mother wit* will tell you when to reveal everything.

If you try to be too sharp, you will cut yourself.

Be genuine in your accomplishments. Don't over- promote yourself. Most people sense that sort of approach and easily recognize you are trying to give yourself additional credit. If you are guilty of too much personal hype, you are damaging yourself in the eyes of others. Let your actions speak for themselves. Don't inflate your ego.

The fool wonders; the wise man asks.

If you are not sure where life is taking you, it's easy to

get lost. Ask for assistance, and don't hesitate to do it. If you take it upon yourself to keep going, without knowing just where you are going, you will run into problems. Taken literally, while in a car, driving off into unknown territory among strangers could be dangerous. So, if you are traveling and get off onto the wrong road, do not go far into unfamiliar ground. Strangers could be just that -- "strange". Wandering through life, or through unknown territory, can be extremely dangerous.

If the teacher is corrupt, the world will be corrupt.

If the teacher is corrupt, the world will be corrupt.

Corruption exists in a great many places. Unfortunately, it can exist with parents, relatives, ministers, church leaders, politicians, and peers. It also may exist within the legal system, medical profession, and our schools. Educators, at any level, have an awesome responsibility to teach what is right. Corruption is not only dangerous, it is a disease which can spread. It is up to each of us to take the first step and help our fellow human beings from going astray. And remember, we are all teaching all the time.

One need not study to become a fool.

There is no school or special training that can stop us

from making absolute fools of ourselves at one time or another. All of us make mistakes in our lives without realizing it. Remember, there is no preparation or study program that will prevent this, even among the most well educated people. There always will be those who try to take advantage of our foolishness. Learn from your mistakes. Don't let foolishness become a way of life or you might deserve to be taken advantage of.

No one needs to plant or cultivate fools; they grow everywhere.

You can find these critical, hailstorm personalities in your family, in church, school, or on the job. You could sit next to them in a fine restaurant or at the theater. They can be destructive, cause chaos, bring trouble. Learn to recognize them and try to interact with groups of a more positive nature.

A good scare is worth more than good advice.

Once a person has lived an experience, the trauma remains, with the mind continually replaying the entire ordeal. When you try to relay this experience to another, it is impossible to give it the impact it had on you. Your words have little or no effect. But, once the other person undergoes a similar traumatic experience, he or she realizes what you were talking about. Some people learn from others' mistakes and some people have to make the mistakes themselves. It all depends on whether or not their *mother wit* is turned on or not. If you remain turned on and tuned in to your *mother wit,* you will benefit from mistakes others make and grow without all the pain caused by your own errors.

Blind in one eye, can't see out of the other.

People who find an excuse to justify everything as they see it are ignoring reality. Chances are pretty good you know people like that. But give them the opportunity to prove their point. Accept suggestions and advice. Try not to shut the doors of your mind. Investigate the possibility that others may be right.

Half empty or half full means the same.

You see things your way, and others see them their way. Perhaps you're both right. There often are two legitimate sides to every discussion, every argument. Who's to say that you're right and they're wrong? The important thing is to open your mind to other opinions. That's what you want from them, isn't it? And, that is faithfulness to good *mother wit*.

All the dirt that doesn't come out in the wash water, will come out in the rinse water.

Secrets that are kept are matters that are not to be discussed. When someone who is important or close to you needs to be told something, it will come out into the open sooner or later. Each cycle will bring the matter out even if you decide not to tell. Some secrets reveal themselves as time goes by. For example, a young girl, under age, claims not to be sexually active and her parents believe her. Then she becomes pregnant. This is the sort of thing that is done in the dark, in secret, that will come to light. If you are true to yourself, you will not have to be secretive about anything of importance.

If you spread the gossip, at least tell the truth

A grapevine can be destructive with wrong information. If you don't have correct, first-hand knowledge then decline the urge to gossip with others. When you are unsure don't be a mud slinger or dirt digger toward someone else. Keep tight lips and opened eyes. Believe more of what you see than what you hear. Then ask questions for clarity. There are two types of language—verbal and non-verbal—that can cross you up. *Mother wit* says, no gossip is better.

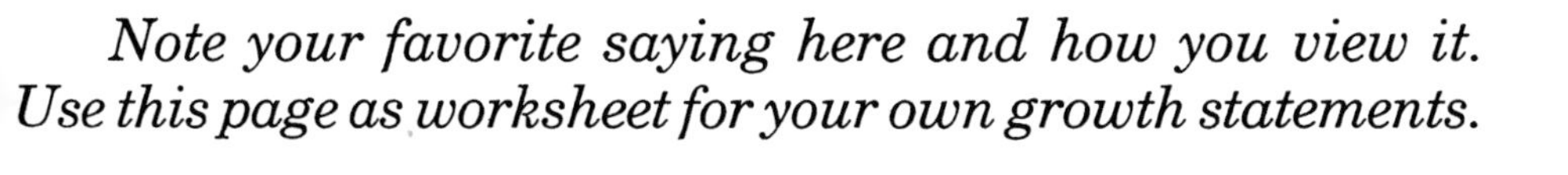

Note your favorite saying here and how you view it. Use this page as worksheet for your own growth statements.

We apologize for the presence of any errors that may have slipped past us in preparing this book. If you have found any errors, please write to us at the address in the back of this book and tell us about them. We want to correct these before our next printing. WIT PUBLISHING

Life and Resolutions

Plan your work, then work your plan.

Set your long- and short-term goals and put them in motion. But be patient. Keep moving at a steady pace toward your intended goal. To achieve your goal may call for sacrifices, but don't slack off. Stick to your plan.

The straw that broke the camel's back.

Enough is enough! Everyone has a breaking point, even though it varies from individual to individual. A person can be pushed only so far before he or she can no longer cope with the pressure. When dealing with individuals, we should be aware that we cannot expect the same result from each person. Don't push so hard that all efforts are wasted because that last push forced someone over the edge.

Every tub must sit on its own bottom.

You have to be responsible to yourself. This is not an overnight achievement. You don't wake up one morning with this outlook on life and have it all together. *Mother wit* is learning precious life skills and putting them to work so you really know you are doing the right thing. Pay attention to the positive and negative signals from others. Remain in control of yourself and success will come.

There are low people in high places.

We have seen this occur too often in politics, but it happens in our everyday lives also. The cream doesn't always rise to the top, and we have to live with the negative results

—results that can affect us in a variety of ways, both good and bad. Just because people achieve lofty positions does not mean everything they say needs to be accepted as the total and complete truth.

It takes less time to do something right than to explain why you did it wrong.

It takes time to make up excuses for your actions or inactions. Down the road, you have to remember what your particular excuse was for your particular action. That takes a lot of scheming. You might slip up and say the wrong thing. When you do things right, life has a clear, even flow. Use your *mother wit* and you won't find yourself in a place where you are constantly justifying errors.

The best place to find a helping hand is at the end of your arm.

Depend on yourself before you ask someone else to do the job for you. Like most things in life, you are most concerned about things that affect you. No one will do it as well as you, because you are looking out for your own interests and have to live with the results.

Debts are the certain outcome of an uncertain income.

Not living on a budget and spending more than you earn creates financial burdens. Then you start "robbing Peter to pay Paul" —taking from one source to cover another. And you get deeper and deeper in debt. Creditors and other legitimate lenders may extend credit, but it will be extremely difficult to climb out of the hole. You must

discipline yourself so your spending habits don't overpower your income. Giving credit where it's due is not always the best way to live. If you are having problems, there are professional organizations that can help you get your financial house in order. But *mother wit* says an ounce of prevention is worth a pound of cure in this case. Being financially responsible is so much better than trying to fix any size money problem.

Be part of the solution, not part of the problem.

If you do not have a resolution to the problem, do not make the problem even more difficult. Find ways to help, not hinder. If you are not going to be a problem-solver, get out of the way. We don't need to inherit even more turmoil.

If the blind lead the blind, both shall fall into a ditch.

When you need others to help you reach a goal or accomplish a task, pick the experienced person, the one who can get straight to the core of the problem. Don't pick the blunderer, the waster of time. Their misguided advice will only steer you further off the track. Look for the individuals who are on track.

If the blind lead the blind, both shall fall into a ditch.

All closed eyes are not sleeping.

Because a person's eyes are shut does not mean he or she is asleep. There are times when you think you are getting away with something, because no one seems to be watching. Whether it's mom or some form of electronic surveillance, those apparently closed eyes know exactly what you're doing.

A watched pot never boils.

A watched pot never boils.

Give a person a chance to breathe. Don't look over someone's shoulder while he or she is working. Put yourself in their shoes. Seems to take forever to finish, doesn't it? Step back and move away. When you come back, the job may be finished. Too often we are not even aware how threatening we may seem to some poor soul who just needs a little time—and privacy—to get the job done.

Keep on your toes, and you won't run down at the heels.

Stay alert and be sensitive. Know where you are going, and remember the way back if you need to return. Be a leader when you can, but be careful of who you follow. Make certain those you follow know where they are going. Spread

your time among your various activities, guarding your mental and physical health. This is where you really can become run down. Stay in touch with your feelings.

The only way someone can ride your back is if you bend over.

"Someone's riding me at work/school/home." Know the feeling? We are not animals created to be ridden. If someone is riding you, determine a way out before the mental and physical strain become worse than the riding itself. Not only will it negatively affect you, your loved ones will be affected also. Chances are, you will bring the problem home. Your entire personality may change; your outlook on life could sour. Try to resolve the situation one-on-one with the person you feel is riding you. Seek a solution that is satisfactory for both of you. If that doesn't work, seek out some higher authority (work/school) or a parent or sibling to help determine a better approach.

The only way someone can ride your back is if you bend over.

Don't throw the baby out with the bath water.

If you are responsible and in charge, pay attention to what you are doing. Make certain that in your haste and rush to finish a task, you don't discard something through carelessness that is very important.

Promptness is the courtesy of kings.

Being on time is a way of life for those who are leaders. It means "I am reliable, dependable, and in charge of my life. I do things the right way. I set the example." You respect such a person, even if you are not a king. You can discipline yourself to be prompt. When you do, you will be called on to play a leadership role because you have shown you respect other people's schedules and you know they have timetables of their own. This kind of courtesy is a big part of *mother wit*.

One who makes excuses accuses himself.

All explanations must be clear and reasonable to your listener. Don't come across with some lame excuse as to why you were unable to do something. This is especially true if you have failed in a situation in which others depended on you. Be considerate of other people's time as well as your own. Do you have a legitimate reason for not fulfilling an obligation? Or is it an excuse? An alibi?

A small leak can sink a great ship.

Whether you're a prominent person or just an average individual, you and your reputation can be ruined overnight. Your most hidden secret can be discovered and change your life forever. Be careful, not only how you live your life, but with whom you share your innermost thoughts. Friendships and relationships can be high-risk if you discover they weren't really your friend. There will be those who hold a grudge for a long time and seek to get even by publicly exposing you for money, for jealousy, for revenge or for the chance to ruin your life.

If you can't beat 'em, join 'em.

There are times when even good ideas are not welcome. It could be lack of interest, poor presentation or even jealousy. Don't beat a dead horse. If you see you can't win a particular battle, don't harbor a grudge. Accept your loss this time, and go along with the group. Learn from your mistakes. Keep trying, and eventually you will win respect and acceptance of your ideas.

Everything comes easier with practice except getting up in the morning.

Don't be in love with sleep. Become more ambitious and stop procrastinating about your plans. When you go to bed, sleep with the thought of getting up and getting started toward your goals. Don't let friends or other pleasures get in your way of your purpose. *Mother wit* will be first to tell you that alarm clocks are plentiful and less costly.

Everything comes easier with practice except getting up in the morning.

Fair exchange is no robbery.

Try to be reasonable when you negotiate. You are not the only person who has needs or must reach a quota. Develop a keen sense for when it is the right time to make your offer and gain acceptance. It will help insure the tran-

sition goes smoothly and that all parties are satisfied with the deal. Closed, sealed, the end—that is the goal. And, when it is truly fair for all concerned, it's *mother wit*.

Priorities and Structure

Crawl before you walk.

Try to achieve success in an orderly manner. Don't race to the top. Take some time and climb the ladder step by step. The race is not always to the swift. If you take your time, once you reach the top, you won't have to turn around to correct mistakes.

Don't put the cart before the horse.

Just think it through, and you'll understand why it doesn't work if you want to move forward. Make certain your priorities are in order. Don't put the wrong things first. Stay with what you know in your *mother wit*, is right. That is what feels right in your heart.

Don't put the cart before the horse.

The high must be built upon the foundation of the low.

Build a firm foundation before you plan to move upward. This holds true for a relationship, family, business, or any commitment that requires structure. If you prepare correctly and build a strong base from the very beginning, it will be in place when you reach the top. Making good use

of your *mother wit* will assure that you will not wobble or fall over. We are talking about a commitment to principles and character here, not about high people or low people. In God's eye we are all equals.

The best way to keep your word is not to give it.

You had all good intentions when you told someone you could fulfill your promise, but unforeseen circumstances prevented you from doing so. The person you promised doesn't care what caused the lack of follow-through. He or she only knows you didn't do what you promised to do. Unfortunately, this could cause bad blood between the two of you. Always be careful about giving your word.

The measure of a person is not the number of servants but the number of people served.

A person is measured by doing for others: by giving, sharing, and helping others achieve what might have seemed impossible. Money in the bank or cars in the garage are not the ways to measure the worth of an individual. You measure a person only by his or her generosity and ways of helping those less fortunate.

There is a time to laugh, a time to cry, a time to play, a time to work, a time to dance, and a time to sing.

This comment, based on the Old Testament, says it very well. Keep things in context. If it's time for business, conduct business. If it's a time to cry, don't try to be the life of

the party. Be in tune with the times and the atmosphere. *Mother wit* rises in each of us and calls us to be responsive to the wonderful old saying, "To every thing there is a season, and a time to every purpose…" and when we are on our true path we do not overlook things and ignore what is going on around us.

Never let yesterday use up too much of today.

Let go of yesterday. The good old days weren't always good. As sure as the sun rises in the east and sets in the west, time moves on. We all re-live the past at some time, remembering what we did wrong and how we could have done better. We lose too much time trying to correct what can no longer be corrected. Make the best of the rest of your life, from this day forward.

It ain't over 'til the fat lady sings.

You haven't won until all the votes have been counted, 'til the final score has been totaled. Wait until the results are final in any of life's little contests. When the election is over; or when the game is finished; or when the race has been won, is the time to celebrate your victory. Then the fat lady can sing—and sing as loud as she wants.

It ain't over 'til the fat lady sings.

Look before you leap.

Watch your step. Be aware of what is going on around you. Make sure it's the right time to make a move. If you hesitate, it may not be time. Don't agree with something unless you understand it fully. Don't sign anything unless you have read it all and understood it. Make certain the way is clear before you move. This is not just a red-light-stop or a green-light-go ordeal, but is a yellow caution light that enables you to slow down, use your *mother wit*, and make sure it is the right time for your decision.

Self-preservation is the first law of nature.

Pay primary attention to yourself and your own needs. It is nobody's responsibility but your own to be in charge of your life. Although they may vary from person to person, we all have essential priorities. They can include self-esteem, social interaction, spirituality, morality, ethical concerns and even financial stability. When you incorporate these priorities into your life and give them the importance they each deserve, you will be on the right track toward taking care of number one. Make yourself the prime concern. You must have high expectations for yourself to be productive. Paying attention to the principles of *mother wit* you will reach your own level of satisfaction and be able to enhance the lives of others.

Relationships and Reality

If the shoe fits, wear it.

Are you being accused of a something you did not do? Are you being described as a type of person you are not? Set the record straight as quickly as you can. Present a rational discussion that legitimately explains your status. If, on the other hand, you did do the deed or you are being described accurately, you'll have to live with that.

If you scatter thorns, don't go barefoot.

Have you made a few enemies along the way, even though it's not your fault? There will always be people who are jealous of success—especially someone else's. That could be the case here. If you cross their path, be careful how you walk . Be ready to protect yourself and your reputation. Seek professional advice if necessary. *Mother wit* will always tell you to watch your step, pray and keep your guard up.

A person can have a mouth that praises and a heart that kills.

"Oh, you look so nice." "I like your hair." "That's a lovely dress." Isn't flattery wonderful? We all know people who mouth the pretty words to your face, and as soon as you turn away would kill you with their looks. If you don't mean something, don't say it. Be sincere. Most people can sense insincerity, whether it is verbal or non-verbal. It's a part of their *mother wit* that keeps them safe.

Yield to a person's taste, and he or she will yield to your interest.

If you are concerned about someone else's happiness, if you care about their problems, and if you take an interest in what he or she is doing and want to get involved, they will be there for you. You share a common interest. Some people are only committed to the degree that, "You look out for me, and I will be there for you." They do it your way in order to get their own way. That's not always a bad situation, but be careful because you could end up with someone else's junk.

A good thing to remember and a better thing to do: Work with the construction gang and not the wrecking crew.

Run with people who are doing positive things—working for peace or a safe environment, for example. Associate with those who are trying to do good in the community, with those who respect their fellow humans and want to be successful in life. The wrecking crew members tear down their lives and try to tear down yours. They are destroyers, not builders. It is your life structure they are affecting.

A problem shared is a problem halved.

When a problem is too much, too large, confide in family members or close friends. If necessary, seek advice and counsel from a professional. Don't be shy about asking for assistance. There are many people struggling with similar personal problems. It is very common to become burdened and not understand, "Why me?" The best response is that

it is not "just you." Open up, and share your feelings and concerns with an interested, yet unbiased, person. It is sound *mother wit* to share the burden because this helps take some of the load off your shoulders.

No one knows the weight of another's burden.

We often commiserate with people experiencing difficult times by telling them, "I know what you are going through. I sympathize, but it's going to be all right." In reality, we may not know the depth of that person's difficulties. Even if we've lived through a similar experience, it's not always the same. Perhaps, instead of just saying, "I know...," we should ask, "How can I help?" But say it only if you mean it and have the time to get involved. This is a way of showing empathy toward people, not just sympathizing with their troubles.

If you love someone, set that person free. If he or she returns, your love is real.

Even when you are apart, your relationship with a loved one should stand solidly. Being away from each other should not create a threatening situation to the relationship. You should be able to be apart without being concerned the other might go astray. Your relationship, bonded with

If you love someone, set that person free. If he or she returns, your love is real.

trust and love, and not affected by distance, is assurance your companion will return regardless of what kind of temptations rise up. The good solid instincts of *mother wit* will tell you if your relationship is real.

When the fog is there, don't pretend it is not; just see the fog.

It's important to accept people for what they have to offer. If you know an individual has a problem, don't shut him or her out of your life. Be a good friend. Acceptance of a persons little differences allows you to learn from all types of teachers. It is much better to work around the problem or ignore it all together than to block the person out of your life. Neither of you gain anything that way.

Two's company. Three's a croud.

Two's company. Three's a crowd.

Always be considerate of others who need time alone or a little "space." If you were not invited or expected somewhere, don't impose by dropping in unannounced. Spare yourself and others any hard feelings by respecting their privacy. It's what you would want! Paying full attention to your own feelings is keeping *mother wit* in the best light and honoring the feelings of others.

People who attend strictly to their own business usually have plenty of business to attend to.

Place value and time on your own affairs. Rule number one is to concern yourself primarily with number one. Concern yourself with your job, home, family, resources, and health. Handle those correctly, and they'll keep you busy enough. You'll have little time to nose into anyone else's affairs. Don't stray in and out of other people's business. Your own well-being is your chief priority. *Mother wit* is knowing when to get involved and when to just "mind your own business".

People who attend to their own business usually have plenty of business to attend to.

You are the apple of my eye and my sweetie pie.

When you hear this, you know you mean a great deal to someone. You bring them joy and happiness, the most satisfying experiences one can have. It reflects a very natural feeling, and there is nothing phony about it. This is a blessing from God. Enjoy this abundance of joy, in all aspects of your life, and at all times of your life.

Absence makes the heart grow fonder.

We all need time away—our space—from that person we often take for granted. A short vacation, even as short as one day, will create a fonder relationship and appreciation and re-kindle the love in our hearts. Use this time to do some soul-searching about the people in your life and return to them with a greater appreciation and consideration of their needs. Such mini-vacations can give each person time for thought and growth.

Misery loves company.

Misery loves company.

There are those who are never happy and seem to never be satisfied. Not only do they tear down those around them, they recruit others to reinforce this negative approach to life. They thrive on bad news and don't ever show a positive side. They always fill the cavity in their minds with unpleasantness. Unfortunately, they are all around us. They cross our path in the church, at home, on the job, and even within the family. Don't let them trap you. We have enough to deal with in our lives without allowing people like this to control us. *Mother wit* shows us how to stay away from negative people and their influences. Everything makes them miserable. Perhaps they need to be steered to professional help, but unless we are qualified, that is not our charge.

Make your enemy your footstool.

Rise above your enemies. Treat them better than they treat you if you wish to get ahead in life. Go around them and take the long way if it is necessary to avoid confrontation. Do not trust their smiling faces. Ignore their helping hands. Do not bare your soul to them because they will try to use that knowledge against you and for their own purposes. Do not let them block your progress as you take positive steps toward your goal. Let your actions, not their attitude, be the challenge.

A smiling face can stab you in the back.

Remember that smiles can be false or deceiving. One is the "business smile." People are trained or asked to smile and be nice so they can sell their product or service to you. Some people smile at everything you say because you have something they want. Beware the con job! On the other hand, there is that natural, genuine person who has a rainbow smile with a heart of gold. Your *mother wit* will help you know the differences in the smiles. Pay close attention and you won't get fooled or hurt.

At times, our tongue and teeth will fall out.

There will be disagreements between loved ones, between parents and children, between sons and daughters, between friends. We must watch what we say with great care. Quickly patch the disagreement with a small bandage, before it becomes a split requiring heavy stitching that may never heal and is sure to leave a scar.

The milk of human kindness never curdles.

When someone shares a kindness with you, it is a heart-warming experience. Yet some people need to have kindness squeezed out of them, like juice from an orange. Let kindness flow from your heart. It is the keystone of a good relationship and absolutely solid *mother wit*. It is amazing how, when we share kindnesses with others, happiness comes back to us in large quantities of kindness from them and everyone.

Success and Prosperity

Success is often hard to take, especially when it's someone else's.

Success is often hard to take, especially when it is someone else's.

People who succeed are either planners or just plain lucky. If we're not planners or lucky, we need to learn to wish them well. And mean it. Jealousy gets us no place. We can waste time crying or complaining about someone else's good fortune, or we can spend our time watching and learning from them and creating a success story for ourselves. Remember, *mother wit* looks for and celebrates the best. Even someone else's success only makes us all feel good, not envy.

People become good through practice rather than by nature.

If you want to be good at whatever you pursue in life, practice will go a long way to making you good. Perhaps you have a talent or gift. Practice doesn't always make perfect, but it does make "better." If you're short on skills, try to improve yourself by taking advantage of seminars, training, classes or through any other program you can afford, and which you feel will help you reach your goal.

Nice guys always finish last.

Some people do wear halos. Let them keep them. There's no reason you can't be nice and finish first. Don't be a doormat. You don't have to be confrontational to insist upon your rights. Let your family, friends and co-workers know where the cutoff is. The best leaders are kind and considerate "nice guys" that know how to finish first. Establish boundaries and stick to them. Limit your empathy.

If you plant bad seeds, you will reep a poor harvest.

If you plant bad seeds, you will reap a poor harvest.

Your children are your seeds. Be their role model. Teach them how to behave and help them develop good character. Instill moral standards in them. Set the standard yourself. Explain the value of their reputation. Introduce them to wholesome habits and lifestyles. They reflect what you invest in them. Take advantage of the wisdom of grandparents by being certain the children establish a relationship with them. Instill common sense in your children, and teach them about life. If you cultivate first, plant the right seeds, and tend them carefully as they sprout, you will have done your best so that your children, your harvest, will blossom into adulthood with full knowledge of *mother wit*.

Reap what you sow.

Do good deeds, and good things will result. They will not necessarily be the result of one specific good deed, but an overall result of all of your positive actions. On the other hand, when you do nasty things to others, nasty things will enter your life. Chances are, bad luck will go hand in hand with the nastiness.

Actions speak louder than words.

Always promising, but never delivering? Words are cheap, but action may not be the real deal for some. Don't talk, do! You've got to deliver. Promises alone are like empty jars, waiting to be filled.

Don't let someone do your thinking for you.

Can't make a decision? Concerned you can't think for yourself? If you need outside help, be careful who you get it from. There are those ready to take you down the wrong path, and be not the least bit concerned if it is the wrong one. It is all right to ask for advice, but you need to make the final decision. And, if you have to make that decision anyway, why not make it in the first place?

Don't let someone do your thinking for you.

My luck is down and out.

At a down time in your life, don't take chances. Events happen in cycles. We've all heard that good or bad events occur in threes. That may be true, but good judgment stands by itself. One support method that may work is to combine common sense with patience. Prayer may help change things, but it's up to you to pay attention to spiritual signs. Remember, it is not just you who is unlucky, so don't be too hard on yourself. We all experience peaks and valleys, ups and downs, good and bad. Sooner or later, things will change if you believe in yourself. That's a beginning. And that's good *mother wit.*

Time heals old pains while creating new ones.

Time heals old pains while creating new ones.

Just because we are healing from yesterday's troubles doesn't mean we won't face new troubles tomorrow. We have no idea what our path through life will bring. But we can shelter ourselves by anticipating some of life's difficulties and shielding ourselves. Pain can a be job loss, physical infirmity, broken family, the trauma of unexpected death. Do your best to overcome the pain and enjoy what you have. A good sense of *mother wit* tells you to take care of your life. You only go around once. So make the best of it in good times and in those times when pain comes along.

What shall it profit anyone, to gain the whole world and lose his or her soul?

Your soul is your own creation. It is a result of the life you lead, and have led. Your character, behavior and reputation; your actions, right or wrong; your achievements, and how they were achieved; the way you established yourself all serve to help separate the good soul from the bad soul. If you can make changes to better your life, do it!

Experience is something you get when you don't get what you wanted.

Experience is something you get when you don't get what you wanted.

We don't always know when we're getting into a good or bad deal. If it turns out to our advantage, we get what we wanted. If it's not to our advantage and turns out to be a bad deal, we still gain something—experience. We can learn from our successes and our failure. You are not the first person, nor will you be the last, not to get what you wanted. Think back carefully to determine just what went wrong. And why did it go wrong? Use the answers from yesterday's experiences to help you with tomorrow's dilemma. This helps build your *mother wit* and prepares you for all future business dealings. It also helps build confidence for all our interpersonal relationships.

He who waits upon fortune is never sure of a dinner.

To wait for your lucky break instead of going out and seeking success is a losing game. Work first for a steady income. Plan a budget to live by and keep within your earnings. Don't depend on luck. If you haven't learned by now, lucky breaks are less than reliable as a means of earning a living. A steady job with a regular paycheck is much less of a gamble and good practice of your *mother wit*.

The early bird catches the worm.

Wake up early, don't linger, and don't procrastinate. If you do, someone is going to get what you want before you do. Remember, you have competition, so be first at the starting gate. Don't be lazy and let your friends or relatives detain you with their own interests. When you are first, you have a better opportunity to achieve your goal. Stay motivated to be in the right place at the right time. You can do it!

Better to eat a dry crust of bread with peace of mind than have a banquet full of trouble.

It's nice not to have to live hand-to-mouth, but what do too many riches bring? Glitter and gold, fancy vehicles, loads of money, famous friends, big-time parties, expensive homes, investments. Nice, but not a way of life for most of us. Especially if you had to walk on a few people to get to the top. Real riches come to those who have a good heart, a good soul, and their health. These make you wealthier than all the money in the world.

Life is like an onion.

It can be sweet or biting. Peel it back slowly, one layer at a time. Sometimes it'll make you cry. Even though there will be a lot of downs in your lifetime, and times when you can't even see light at the end of a tunnel, don't give up. Don't develop an onion-skin. Become thick-skinned and work through life. It doesn't have to be all tears and sadness. *Mother wit* says, sometimes life, like an onion, tastes very sweet.

Notes for the reader.

This page is another for your additions. Perhaps here you might like to try adding a little drawing of your own like the Apple Characters created to help you envision the thoughts and commentaries. Be creative. You can do it. Add a new saying and then increase your memory of it with your own artwork.

Thrift and Investment

A bird in the hand is worth two in the bush.

You physically have something in your possession and decide you want another "something." You must have it, even if it's not easy to obtain. Before you go grabbing for an extra, hold on to what you have. When you greedily reach for the new, you could drop the old and end up with nothing.

Creditors have better memories than debtors.

Creditors have better memories than debtors.

Miss a payment and get ready to be on notice. Even though most creditors will pursue you in a civilized progression -- notifying you by phone, in writing, certified mail -- it could finally end in the courts. And you don't want your problem to get that far. The creditor wants to be repaid and is justified in seeking repayment. Some creditors can be very understanding and will work with you to resolve the debts. If you do have a problem, take the initiative and contact the creditor. Stay in touch and remember who you talk to. Write down names and dates and request that special arrange-

ments be put in writing. Most of all, keep in touch. Remember that you are only a phone call away. Don't make your creditors chase you! You'll have peace of mind instead of feeling harrassed.

Never beg for that which you have the power to earn.

If you ever are going to earn a living, you'll have to put an end to the attitude that someone else can do it for you. Learn to manage what you have. Don't overspend what you earn because if you do, you'll be up the creek without a paddle. Begging is a sign of irresponsibility, of laziness. There is an old story about the ant and the grasshopper. The ant worked hard during the summer, and the grasshopper did nothing but play and hop from stalk to stalk. During the summer, the ant stored food. The grasshopper lived for today. When the harsh winter came, the ant stayed in out of the cold and survived. The lazy, unprepared grasshopper perished in the cold weather. If you are wise, you will be like the ant—work hard and care for yourself. Resolve that your own self-reliance will provide you with the items necessary for survival. Nobody will do it for you.

Investigate before you invest.

Get totally involved with your project. Ask questions and make inquiries to determine if the project is worthwhile, has value, and that you haven't overlooked anything. You don't want to put money and time into a losing endeavor. Seek advice from a reputable resource person or firm. Don't forget that nothing is surefire. Even after you investigate, you could be in for disappointment. Good *mother wit* tells you to make sure you are totally prepared, financially and mentally.

Kept records mean you have the facts.

Documents are very important. Hold on to receipts, invoices, notes and statements. It's a great deal easier to make your point and win your case when you have supportive documentation to back you up. When you make a purchase, check the receipt to make certain such things as company rules—no refund, return in thirty days or no exchange, not returnable—are listed. Knowing these things up front gives you the option to buy or not to buy. Keep in mind that many company policies are posted around the store and may not be on a sales receipt. If you do not understand the store policy, ask questions before you buy.

A stitch in time saves nine.

When you see a problem coming, face it head on and take care of it right away. Save yourself the headache of trying to resolve it after it's out of control. It'll take more time to get it back right, and it may cost more in aggravation and money. Save yourself time by staying on top of things as they arise.

He who died too rich lived too poor.

You can't take it with you! Your wealth and assets cannot be transferred to the hereafter. But there are many worthwhile organizations that could use financial assistance. Think about contributing to them. You may want to express yourself by putting some of what you gained back into the community. It shouldn't take a plaque on the wall or a building named after you to consider such assistance. What better way to show your appreciation? What better way to show you lived your life by the ever-important principles of *mother wit*?

Looking for a needle in a haystack.

Losing or misplacing something, whether it's valuable or not, is very frustrating. It takes time and patience to search for it. Put sentimental objects and valuables somewhere safe. But use your *mother wit* to remember where you put them. The difficulty of finding one single needle in a normal-sized haystack points up the problem.

Looking for a needle in a haystack.

Thoughts and Reflections

Would you? Could you? Should you? Did you...?

Any of these actions might have made a difference, but you chose not to do any of them. If someone who had been drinking was going to drive, *should you* have taken the keys? *Could you* have driven them home? *Should you* have asked them to sleep over? *Would you* have made the difference in preventing a tragedy? You don't want to be the one saying these things about a loved one, friend, or acquaintance. Consider the alternatives before you're sorry about an incident you would have, could have, or should have prevented.

The grass is always greener on the other side of the fence.

Get facts to support any change you might be considering because someone else seems to be doing an absolutely great job. Do some research into your new project. Remember, what you are doing now may be just as positive as any change. All that glitters isn't necessarily gold. *Mother wit* tells us to always be grateful for what we have and not worry about someone else.

The grass is always greener on the other side of the fence.

Once burned, twice warned.

I trusted you. I loaned you money, put you up when you had no place to stay. I fed you when you were hungry. Then you deceived me, lied to me. You didn't keep your word. Now you ask me to do you another favor. "No can do". It was my decision to help you; it was your decision to turn on me. Get out! You're history! This may seem harsh or cruel but it's good use of *mother wit* to take care of yourself. Sometimes taking good care of yourself is leaving inconsiderate people behind. People who lie or deceive others are not being fair and good *mother wit* always considers what is best for all persons concerned, including yourself.

Don't burn your bridges behind you.

Don't burn your bridges behind you.

Someone has helped you reach a certain amount of success. Now you feel you don't need that person any more, and slam the door in his or her face. The day will come when that door has to swing back the other way. The person you need—again—now is on the outside. Move on in life in such a way that if you need to, you can go back. Then your friend could welcome you and help re-open the door. You want to be honored by those you have helped, and *mother wit* tells you to always remember those who helped you.

Don't cut off your nose to spite your face.

Do not mistreat or overlook someone who is an asset to you in order to gain someone else's approval. If you feel there will be a conflict between the two, be careful how you break your relationship to start another. If you have a relationship that has worked well for you, make peace. Keep your options open for the future. *Mother wit* never allows us to hurt ourselves in our efforts to grow.

Don't count your chickens before they hatch.

You cannot be certain of something you do not have. Don't make definite plans for indefinite possibilities. Maybe there is some money you have been promised. Be mindful not to have spent it before it actually gets into your hands. Wait until you physically have what is due you before you count on all that it can do for you.

Don't count your chickens before they hatch.

Don't jump from the frying pan into the fire.

Don't jump from one problem to an even larger one in the hope you're going to find all your answers. If you are going to make a change, don't make it just for the sake of change itself. *Mother wit* tells you to think it through before you make that giant leap.

You don't miss the water 'til the well runs dry.

"Absence" means not there...gone...not present. The loss of a job and income are materialistic absences. Loss of a loved one or the breakup of a romance are non-materialistic absences. You have to determine what is most important to you. If it's an object, protect it from loss. If it's a human being, love, respect, and share with that person. Then, if there is a loss, an absence, you will have the most treasured memories. Sometimes losses are unavoidable and those treasured memories will help you move on to new experiences.

Chalk up a disappointment as an experience to be forgotten.

Unhappy the decision didn't go your way? You didn't win the argument or the election or even get to choose the movie you wanted to see? Maybe you are not happy about the outcome. Perhaps you were right, and the others were wrong. But no one saw it your way. Now, you've exhausted all your avenues or means of satisfaction. Drop it! Let it rest forever. We all have been disappointed at one time or another, and each of us has suffered when others were not right or fair. At least we thought they weren't. Do not let a losing battle affect you so negatively. Experience is usually, but not always, the best teacher.

As we get angry, we fall into error.

Angry? That means you can't think well. You don't listen. You act without thinking. The world's against you. You are not in control. If you should err when you're out of control, when you're angry, there most likely will be a nega-

tive result. Only you can decide if the error is worth the penalty. How do you bring yourself under control? You can "count to ten," "take a break to cool off," or "just walk away." Remember the consequences of acting in anger. You may not be the only one who will suffer.

Men don't carry tissue. They cry inside.

The feelings of men are very much alive but very much camouflaged. As time goes by, men are getting in touch with their feelings and learning to express them. Masking of a man's feelings was taught because showing tears was a sign of weakness. Today it is a sign of reality and it flushes away some of the unhappiness and isolative pain. The *mother wit* part of this is that women are understanding that men have a difficult time displaying their feelings and are helping them. And the men are coming to terms with their softer side.

I often have regretted my response, but not my closed mouth.

Learn to say "No comment." At least keep the expression in mind, even if you don't utter it. If you are not sure you can respond without tripping over your tongue, keep your mouth shut. If you must say something, try "Let me get back to you." Take time to think the matter over and get an idea of what you wish to say. You don't want to put your foot in your mouth. A closed mouth can save you later embarrassment. Be tactful when you talk, or you will be sorry you were not.

Pick up the pieces
and get on with your life.

Feel as though your life has been tumbling downhill? Can't seem to get back on track? Even if you feel that way, don't roll over and die. Don't quit! There is always a second chance or another option. Seek assistance from family, friends, or neighbors. If it's a minor problem, you may be able to fix it quickly. A major situation may take some time to resolve, but continue to work on your problem. Snap back to reality. Pick up the broken pieces and put them back together by "sticking" to it. Remember, you are not alone. There are others who depend on you.

It is better to teach a child well
than to repair him or her as an adult.

Start the discipline when they are below your knees. Teach them first, the separation between parent and child. Let them know you are the authority figure in their lives. Have a set of rules, introduce values, teach trust and respect. Teach love and devotion. Praise when there is superbness. Discipline when there has been sour behavior. Parents or guardians should be in step with each other's thoughts and stand firm on corrective actions with consistency. Work with each other, not against each other. Teach the strong principles of *mother wit* and your child will grow up with love, respect and high self esteem which will be a reward for both the child and the parents.

One final thought...

I am not afraid of tomorrow
for I have seen yesterday,
and I love today.

Author unknown

About the Author

Mrs. Henry Jean Carter was born in Perry, Georgia. She has lived in Washington D.C. and attended school there. After graduating from High School in her home town as Miss Senior High and a very popular girl, Mrs. Carter moved to Cleveland, Ohio. She is married and has a family that she is in love with. She has a wonderful sense of humor which will become apparent to you as you read on.

The author has attended Cuyahoga Community College, Dyke College, Sawyer Business College and Barbizon School of Modeling where she learned professional poise and attitude to match her career skills.

Mrs. Carter has worked for Cuyahoga County Juvenile Court, as an advocate and as a volunteer in the Juvenile Detention Home school system. She has also been a volunteer for the Cleveland Free Clinic, as a fund raiser. Mrs. Carter works for the Med-Surg department of a major hospital. This is her first book. She plans to continue writing self help books and continue to discover additional creative writing talent.

Mrs. Carter plans to animate the apple family featured in this book for short television spots for children's programing and use as "Thought-for-the-day" public service announcements.

The author wrote this book to relive and share some of the best knowledge about *mother wit* and to spread it to those who are not familiar with the subject. She says it represents her finger print in life to share with all nationalities and generations. It is her fond hope that each reader will benefit from this text book when lifes hurdles arise in front of them.

Mrs. Carter learned from many of these lessons during her lifetime. She offers these words to enhance your journey through life and the circumstances you will encounter.

Henry Jean has been collecting sayings, witticisms, puns and aphorisms for many years and does not know the original source of many of the phrases offered in this writing. She feels confident that the originators would not require recognition as much as the words need to be passed on to all who read them. Many of these messages found a willing student in the author and have influenced her life directly.

The author feels this book will help readers to think; will recapture the memory of the *mother wit* common sensibilities that were taught (or learned through mistakes).

The illustrations are here to make you laugh and to help you see more clearly the meaning analyzed. The apple family is throughout the book as a cast of characters with talent to help create understanding for readers.

I would be honored
if you would like to share
comments, experiences or other sayings with me
that have been important and helpful
in your life.
Please address letters to:

Mrs. Henry Jean Carter
Wit Publishing
P.O. Box 221105
Beachwood, Ohio 44122

You may also use the above address
for information about up-coming book signings
and speaking engagements.
Thank you!

To make arrangements for book signings,
or to schedule speaking engagements,
or to order additional copies of
The Teachings of Mother Wit
Please Call: 1-800-537-1030

or write to:

Fairway Press
P.O. Box 4503
517 S. Main Street
Lima, Ohio 45802-4503

How to Order

You may copy this page for ordering!

The Teachings of...Mother Wit by Henry Jean Carter

Make Check or money order
payable to **Wit Publishing**.

Quantity_____ at $14.00 each............................ $________
Ohio residents add 7% sales tax ($.98 per book) ________
In Canada the Cost is $16.00 (no sales tax)
Plus shipping and handling $3 first book.......... ________
$1 each additional book... ________
Total amount of check or money order.............. ________

Address where we should send the book(s):
Name____
Address______________________________________
City_________________________State___________Zip________
and mail to: **Wit Publishing**
P.O. Box 221105
Beachwood, Ohio 44122

To order additional copies by credit card
Please call: 1-800-537-1030 or write to **Fairway Press**
P.O. Box 4503
517 S. Main Street
Lima, Ohio 45802-4503

☐ **VISA** ☐ **MasterCard**

Card No.________________________________
Expiration Date__________________________

Signature (Required)______________________________